GO AND TELL JESUS.

BY

OCTAVIUS WINSLOW, D.D.,

BATH,

AUTHOR OF "MIDNIGHT HARMONIES," "THE PRECIOUS THINGS OF GOD," ETC.

"I am better acquainted with JESUS than with any friend I have on earth."—HEWITSON.

FROM THE 75th ENGLISH EDITION.

NEW-YORK:

A. D. F. RANDOLPH & CO.,

770 BROADWAY.

1869.

GO AND TELL JESUS.

"AND his disciples came and took up the body and buried it, *and went and told Jesus.*"—MATTHEW 14 : 12.

As if to illustrate the nature and test the efficacy of His great and gracious expedient of saving sinners, it pleased the redeeming God that the *first* subject of death should be a believer in the Lord Jesus. Scarcely had the righteous Abel laid his bleeding lamb upon the altar—that altar and that lamb all expressive of the truth, and radiant with the glory of the person and work of the coming Savour — ere he was called to seal with his blood the faith in Christ he had professed. But if the first victim, he was also the first victor He fell by death, but he fell a con queror of death. He lost the victory, but he won the battle. Thus was the "last enemy" foiled in his very *first* assault upon our race. The point of his lance was then turned, the venom of his sting was then impaired, and, robbed of his prey, he saw in the pale and gory form his shaft had laid low the first one of that glorious race of confessors, that "noble army of martyrs," who in all succeeding ages should overcome sin, hell, and death, by the blood of the Lamb.

It was on an occasion similar to the death of the first martyr, that the passage suggesting the subject of these pages was written. Falling a sacrifice to his fidelity, as Abel had to his faith, John was now a mangled corpse — the victim of Herod's sin and cruelty. Taking up the headless body of their master, the disciples of John bore it to the tomb, and then went and poured their tale of woe into the ear, and laid their crushing sorrow upon the heart of Jesus. "*And his disciples came and took up the body and buried it,* AND WENT AND TOLD JESUS." It was, perhaps, their first direct communication with the Saviour. They had known but little of Jesus until now. Another being had engaged their interest, and occupied their thoughts. Absorbed in their admiration of the star that heralded its approach, they had scarcely caught sight of the Sun which had just appeared above the horizon. In vain had John, with characteristic lowliness, reminded them that he was not the Messiah, and but

His forerunner. Wedded to their master, they thought of, clung to, and loved only him. John must therefore die—the star paling and disappearing before the deepening splendor of the divine ascending Orb. All this was the ordering of infinite wisdom and love. The removal of John was necessary to make his disciples better acquainted with Jesus. They had heard of Him, had seen Him, and in a measure believed in Him ; but they never fully knew or loved Him until now that profound grief brought them to His feet. What a Divine Saviour, what a loving Friend, what a sympathizing Brother Jesus was! how truly human in His affinities, compassionate in His heart, gentle in His spirit! they had no adequate conception until the surge of sorrow flung them upon His sympathy. Ah!

how they clung to Jesus now! Owning no other master, seeking no other friend, repairing to no other asylum in their lonely grief, "*they went and told Jesus.*" Favored disciples! honored men! Oh! how many now hymning their praises in heaven, or still watering their couch with tears on earth, will alike testify that until God smote the earthly idol, or broke the human staff, or dried up the creature spring, Jesus was to them as an unknown Saviour and Friend. Blessed, thrice blessed sorrow that leads us to Jesus! That sorrow—dark, deep, though it be—will wake the harp of the glorified to heaven's sweetest melody. The bitterest grief of the saint on earth will issue in the sweetest joy of the glorified in heaven — because that grief, sanctified by the Spirit, brought the heart into a closer alliance and sympathy with Him who was emphatically a "man of sorrows and acquainted with grief."

We know so much of divine truth, my reader, as we have in a measure a personal experience of it in our souls. The mere speculatist and notionalist in religion is as unsatisfactory and unprofitable as the mere theorist and declaimer in science. For all practical purposes both are but ciphers. The character and the degree of our spiritual knowledge begins and terminates in our knowledge of Christ. *Christ* is the test of its reality, the measure of its depth, and the source of its growth. If you are advancing in an experimental, sanctifying acquaintance with the Lord Jesus, you are advancing in that knowledge which Paul thus estimates: "I count all things but loss for the excellency of the knowledge of

Christ Jesus my Lord." Dear reader, let the chief object of your study be to know the Lord Jesus. It may be in the region of your sinfulness, emptiness, weakness, and foolishness that you learn Him—nevertheless, however humiliating the school, slow the progress, and limited the attainment, count every fresh step you make in a personal acquaintance with the Lord Jesus as a nobler triumph, and as bringing you into the possession of more real wealth than were the whole arcana of human knowledge and science mastered, and its untold treasures poured at your feet. When adversity comes — when death approaches — when eternity unveils — oh! how indescribably valuable, how inconceivably precious will then be *one* faith's touch, *one* faith's glimpse of a crucified and risen Saviour! All other attainments then vanish, and the only knowledge that abides, soothes, and comforts, is a heart-felt acquaintance with the sublimest fact of the Gospel, that "*Christ Jesus came into the world to save sinners.*' Oh! whatever other studies may engage your thoughts, forget not, as you value your eternal destiny to study the Lord Jesus Christ.

Intercourse with Jesus.

The subject which we must keep prominent before us is: *Intercourse with Jesus.* That there may exist a serious defect in the experience of many Christians touching this point, we solemnly believe. There is in the walk of many so wide a chasm between Jesus and their personal and confidential fellowship, as to leave upon the mind the conviction that they have no dealings with Jesus at all! Hence the distressing doubts, the timid fears, the obscure evidences, the beclouded hopes, that shade the lustre, impair the vigor, and render dubious the religion of so many. The secret is, *they have so little to do with Jesus!* and, as a natural result, Jesus, in the bestowment of His favors, in the manifestations of Himself, in the breathings of His love, has so little to do with them! Oh! how sad, that such distance and coldness should ever exist between Christ and a soul redeemed with his most precious blood! What an evidence of the fallen condition of our humanity, and of its but partial sanctification, even in its renewed state.

We propose, in the further unfolding of this interesting subject, to state the *grounds* upon which the believer is warranted to gc and tell Jesus—the *occasions* on which he is privileged to go and tell Jesus —and the *blessings* that will flow from his going and telling Jesus.

The first springs *from what Jesus is Himself.* The very fact that He whom we approach—the Being, the Saviour, the Friend with whom this close and constant intercourse is maintained—is JESUS, forms our highest encouragement, our divinest warrant. It is not every great person who is at all times accessible. The official barriers which surround, or the austere address which marks him, may interdict and discourage all free and confidential approach. It is not so with Jesus. Infinitely great though He is—for He is the Maker of all beings and worlds—there is not a being in the universe so accessible as Jesus. We approach Him, and we find Him—sin only excepted—

a being just like ourselves. His divine nature is clad with the human—His circumstances are human—His love is human—His sympathy is human—His compassion is human—His smile is human—His trials, temptations, sufferings, and sorrows, are human; all are so human that there is not a petition with which we approach, growing out of our suffering *humanity*, that challenges not a hearing, that awakens not a response. Let us add a few particulars. Do we go to Him burdened?—we are in the presence of Him who bore the mighty weight of sin. Do we go to Him in sorrow?—we are in the presence of Him who was acquainted with grief. Do we go to Him in tempation?—we are in the presence of Him who was tempted in all points like as we are. Carry we to His feet our adversities, poverty, want?—we are holding audience with Him who, when He sojourned on earth, was poor, homeless, and unbefriended—who subsisted by charity, and had not where to lay His head. And, then, there is another encouragement to our approach growing out of His *official* relations—they are all in our favor. His prophetical office—His priesthood—His royal character, all have a relation to our varied need. Exalted as His position is, each separate office that He fills warrants and invites our approach. And, as if to crown the encouragements accumulating around our access to Jesus, there are His own personal attractions—all-inviting and irresistible. Every thing in the *person* of Jesus encourages our advance. Does glory charm us—does beauty attract us—does love win us—does gentleness subdue us—does sympathy soothe us—does faithfulness inspire confidence?—then, all this is in Jesus, and all invites us to draw near. He is the "altogether lovely," and if our minds can appreciate the grand, and our hearts are sensible of the tender; if they feel the power of that which is superlatively great and exquisitely lovely, then we shall need no persuasion to arise, and go and tell Jesus every emotion of our souls, and every circumstance of our history. Take all that is tender in love—all that is faithful in friendship—all that is wise in counsel—all that is long-suffering in patience, all that is balmy, soothing, and healing in the deepest sympathy—and its embodiment, its impersonation is—JESUS. Can we, then, be insensible to all this personal attraction, and hesitate repairing to His feet—telling Him all? In addition to what Jesus is in Himself, there is the encouragement to repair to Him growing out of the *covenant relations* He sustains to His people. Apart from His ever-loving heart, kindly disposition, and sympathizing nature, Jesus is your Brother, your Friend, your Goel, next of kin. As a Brother, He knows the need of His brethren in adversity; as a Friend, He showeth Himself friendly; and as next of kin, He has redeemed your soul, and bought back your lapsed inheritance. Nay, more, He is your Advocate in heaven, your Intercessor at the right hand of God, your Representative, having ascended up on high to take possession of heaven on your behalf, and to prepare a place for you. Upon His heart He wears your name—a precious pearl in the priestly breastplate. And there is not a moment of time, nor an event of life, nor a circumstance of daily history, nor a mental or spiritual emotion, in which you are not borne upon the love, and remembered in the ceaseless intercession of Christ. Is not this enough? What more, to win you to His feet in all the endearing confidence of one who delights in every thing, to go and tell Jesus? Is there another being in the universe you can approach with such perfect repose of mind, with such full assurance of heart, with an unveiling of every thought, emotion, and feeling, so full, unreserved, and confiding? No! not one!

His Mediatorial Work.

The mediatorial work of the Lord Jesus constitutes another and assured ground of our approach.

The full, complete, and free salvation which He by His obedience and death has accomplished for sinners, anticipates every objection, and answers every argument growing out of our personal and deep unworthiness. Nothing can withstand this plea. When we enter into His presence—be it as a sinner confessing guilt—be it as a penitent supplicating pardon — be it as a mourner unveiling sorrow—be it as needy asking grace—or, be it as a recipient of mercy offering the sacrifice of praise — we stand upon the basis of an Atonement which meets our case in its most peculiar form. It is utterly impossible that we can be repulsed. We approach Jesus *by Jesus!* We "take hold of His strength," and a rejection of our suit must involve a rejection of Himself. We draw near by the way of His cross. We penetrate into His loving heart through His pierced side. His wounds are our "door of hope." We plead His own merits — bathe in His own blood—enfold us in His own righteousness—and the one name that breathes from our lips in its purest fragrance and sweetest music is, His own! — that "name which is above every name." Can he deny us? Will He reject us? Impossible! How shall we more strongly put the case? What more can we add to annihilate all your doubt and fear touching your reception, if you but arise and come to Jesus? Tell me after this statement—justified and borne out by every sentence of revealed truth—who shall dare interpose or come between your soul and Christ? What echoes of the "law's loud thunder," what lightning gleams of justice, what profound sense of sinfulness, what aggravated departures, shall presume to interdict your approach to the Saviour! The Cross of Calvary clasped within the arms of faith, you may challenge the universe to forbid your approach to Jesus—every foe shall turn pale and shrink away. No sin, no curse, no Satan can stand beneath the sacred, solemn shadow of that cross where—impaled, suffering, dying—hung the incarnate God. Sooner at the bidding of a mortal shall the laws of nature stand still, and this universe cease to be; sooner shall Christ vacate His throne of glory, and God resign the government of all worlds and of all beings, than shall a poor penitent, humble, supplicating soul enter into the presence of Jesus, pleading His own infinite merits and most precious blood, be chilled by coldness, be awed by a frown, or be rejected with disdain. Once more, believing reader, would we remind you that Jesus your Surety Head has done all for you, and has left you nothing to do but go and tell Him all. He has paid all your great debt, annihilated all your innumerable sins, exhausted every particle of your tremendous curse, and is now set down at the right hand of God to secure by His intercession, and to administer by His government, the untold blessings purchased by His blood—can you then hesitate and demur? Approach Him, and with the gentlest pressure of faith, touch the spring of His heart's love, and every door flies open to welcome you.

The Divine Relationship.

In addition to all this, we have to blend the thought of the close and sacred *relationship* which binds you to Jesus, on the ground of which you are emboldened to approach and tell Him all. As a believer, you are one of the countless number given by the Father to Jesus. You are one of His sheep, His brother, His friend. To receive you with indifference, or to repulse you with scorn, would be to trample upon Himself—for we are as His brethren, "bone of his bone and flesh of his flesh." In us, too, He beholds His Father's image restored, His own righteousness imputed, and our bodies living temples of the Holy Ghost. When the eye of King Ahasuerus lighted upon Esther, robed and jewelled with royal splendor, her person found grace in his sight, and he bade her approach. With a complacency and delight infinitely transcending this, does Jesus contemplate the believer as he enters into the Divine presence, comely with His comeliness put upon him. Extending the symbol of welcome, He invites your approach; His heart, responsive to your petition, is prepared, and His power, commensurate with your case, is "able to do exceeding abundantly above all that we ask or think." O royal highway of access! Opened by the blood and kept open by the intercession of Christ, the much incense of whose merit ascendeth up moment by moment before the throne —there is not a thought, a feeling, or a circumstance, with which you may not go and tell Jesus.

"Just as I am—Thy love unknown
Hath broken every barrier down,
Now to be Thine, yea, Thine alone,
O Lamb of God! I come!"

Let me remind you, in vindication of the glory of Immanuel, that going and telling Jesus, implies on His part, no ignorance of, or indifference to your case. He who redeemed us is God—"God manifest in the flesh." All persons, all things, all events are known to Him from the end to the beginning. When, therefore, you stand in the presence chamber of Jesus you prefer no request, breathe into His ear no sorrow, unveil to His eye no infirmity, with which, in all its most minute detail, He was not already infinitely better acquainted than yourself. Long ere the sadness had shaded your brow, or a tear had dimmed your eye, or the burden had pressed your spirit, or the perplexity had woven its web around your path, or the archer had bent his bow and winged his shaft—Jesus knew it all, had appointed it all, had anticipated it all. It was no surprise to Him! Precious truth! Christ had entwined my perplexity with His thoughts, had wrapped my grief around His heart, had provided a pavilion for my safety ere a pebble had paved, or a cloud had shaded, or a whisper of the storm had breathed over my path. "O Lord! thou knowest my downsitting and mine uprising; thou understandest my thoughts afar off, thou compassest my path and my lying down, and art acquainted with all my ways." Satisfied with such a fact, cheered by such a truth, animated by such a thought, you may unhesitatingly advance into the unknown history of another year; firm in the belief that Jesus will be faithful in fulfilling the promise, "I will bring the blind by a way that they knew not; I will lead them in paths that they have not known; I will make darkness light before them, and crooked things straight. These things will I do unto them, and not forsake them."

Let me now briefly trace a few of the many *occasions* in which you are invited to avail yourself of this privilege.

Is Sin a Burden?

Are you burdened with a sense of sin? Go and tell Jesus. There is no burden that mortal ever bore like this! Feel you this weight? Then there is spiritual sensibility, a holy consciousness, a divine life in your soul. This is not the mark of an unconverted nature. The corpse recoils not from its own corruption, nor is the rock sensible of its own weight. You feel yourself a sinner, your spirit is contrite for sin, your heart is broken for sin, your whole soul is bowed in the dust of self-abhorrence for sin. Then, my reader, there is life, spiritual, divine, deathless life in your soul; and you are just the one *to go and tell Jesus.* To whom can you repair with that burden, to whom confess that sin, to whom unveil that guilt but—JESUS? As a sinner you need a Saviour—Jesus is your Saviour. As guilty, you desire to know how God can pardon, justify, and accept you—Jesus, "the brightness of the Father's glory, and the express image of his person," is prepared to reconcile you to God, and thus bring you into perfect peace. "Being justified by faith we have peace with God, through our Lord Jesus Christ." Appointed by God, Jesus is the infinite burden-bearer of our race. "Surely he hath borne our griefs and carried our sorrows. He was wounded for our transgressions, he was bruised for our iniquities." That burden you feel Jesus bore, for that sin you mourn Jesus suffered, for that iniquity you acknowledge Jesus bled—for that guilt, beneath which you tremble, Jesus died. Go, then, and tell Jesus all your sin. To whom can you tell it but to Him? He "came into the world to save *sinners*." "Christ died for the *ungodly*." His "blood cleanseth from *all* sin." His "name is JESUS because he *saves*." To Him confess all your sin. Beneath His cross, watering His feet with tears of penitence, acknowledge your transgressions—unveil your every sin. He knows it all, yet would have you tell Him all; withholding, veiling, extenuating nothing. Only go and tell Jesus *what* a sinner you are, and that you are emboldened thus to come because He has revealed Himself as *such* a Saviour; that it is His pardoning mercy—His boundless love—His gracious invitation—His tender, compassionate heart, that never yet rejected a seeking sinner, that warrants your coming, that draws and woos you to His feet. Oh! if instead of brooding over your unworthiness, magnifying your sins, and lessening His most free grace to sinners, you will but arise and go and tell Jesus, the song of the pardoned would soon burst in the sweetest melody from your lips. Only go to Jesus—

"With all your sins against your God,
All your sins against His laws,
All your sins against His blood,
All your sins against His cause—
Sins as boundless as the sea!
And hide them in Gethsemane!"

Are You Going Back?

Go and tell Jesus your backslidings. "My people are bent to backsliding from me," is the mournful language of God. "Our backslidings are many," is the penitential acknowledgment of the Church. Backsliding, as the simple definition of the word intimates, is *a going back.* "They have gone backward and not forward," says the Lord. How constantly do we recede in the ways of the Lord Jesus. And if, through restraining grace, there are no outbreaks of sin, there yet may be the secret declension of the soul, the hidden backsliding of the heart, all concealed from human eye, yet "open to the eye of him with whom we have to do." Oh! how little *vital* religion, how little of the anointing of the Holy Ghost, of the power of real godliness, is there in the souls of many who yet at the Lord's table solemnly profess themselves His! Perhaps, my reader, you are awakened to a sense of your backsliding from the Lord. Startled by the discovery, alarmed at the symptoms, deploring the consequences, you exclaim: "Oh! that it were with me as in days that are passed, when the candle of the Lord shone round about me." You think of the "love of your espousals;" of your "song in the days of your youth, in the day when you came up out of the land of Egypt;" of the "green pastures and the still waters," and your heart dies within you. Be it so—be it that you have wandered far from God, and that you have fallen by your iniquity; that you have pierced afresh the bosom of that Saviour that has so often pillowed your head in weakness and grief; yet, go and tell Jesus! There is not in the universe a being who can so understand and sympathize with your case as He. Tell Him how your affections have strayed—how your love has chilled—how the spirit of prayer has waned in your soul, and what ascendency the world, the creature, and self have obtained in your mind. Take with you words and turn to the Lord, say unto Him: "Take away all iniquity, and receive us graciously."

In this connection of our remarks, we would venture upon an observation which relates closely to the happy and holy walk of the child of God. How many a believer in Jesues pursues his Christian course with a sad countenance, the reflection of a yet sadder heart, from the consciousness of the indwelling evil of his nature perpetually exhibiting itself in flaws, and failure, and dereliction, to which the eye of human affection is blind, but which to his own inspection are real, palpable and aggravated—not the less humiliating and abhorrent because unknown and unsuspected by all but himself. The remedy, what is it? *Going and telling Jesus!* Oh! if there be one view of this privilege more precious, endearing, and sacred than another, it is the liberty of admitting Jesus to the deepest confidence of the heart, of unveiling to him thoughts, imaginations, and emotions, which no inducement could persuade us to reveal to our most dear and intimate friend. Bending beneath the cross, the eye reposing in faith upon the Crucified, there is no heart-wandering, no mental emotion, no secret so profound, no sorrow so delicate, no perplexity so great, no guilt so aggravated which the lowly, penitent heart may not fully and freely tell Jesus. It is the oversight of this truth that produces so much solitary grief in the minds of many of the Lord's people. They forget *what* a Friend, *what* a Brother, *what* a Confident, *what* a Saviour they have in Jesus. They refuse to go and tell Him all; and thus, brooding over their failures and sins, nursing in loneliness their trials and sorrows, their "sore runneth in the night, and their soul refuseth to be comforted."

Are you Walking in Darkness?

As a child of the light walking in darkness—go and tell Jesus. The path of the believer, though it be the only sunny path in life, is often shaded and dreary. There are spiritual despondencies and mental depressions peculiar to the divine life of a Christian. If the "Sun of Righteousness" had His periods of obscuration, His temporary eclipse when His whole soul was enshrouded in deep gloom, it is no great marvel that along a similar shaded path His disciples should travel. The cloud that envelops you may be so dense as to obscure every star, and to extinguish every ray. You can not see Jesus, you can not descry a single promise upon which you can rest your soul, not a word of Jesus from which you can extract comfort or gather hope. All means fail, and every spring of consolation is dried, and you have no evidence of your interest in the Saviour, of your adoption into His family, of your title to glory — and you exclaim: "My God! my Father! why hast thou forsaken me?" But, hush that murmur! God has not forsaken you. "O Israel! thou shalt not be forgotten of me," is His assuring declaration. What is your course?

Go and tell Jesus! If in the universe there is one who can sympathize with this spiritual darkness it is He. Turn you in faith to the full sunshine of this Divine Orb. In Christ's light you shall see light upon all the hidden riches and glory of the kingdom of God within you. Sinful though you are, your soul, renewed and inhabited by the Holy Ghost, presents the pencilings and enshrines the gems of a Divine Artist, the beauty, grandeur, and costliness of which are hidden until Jesus shines upon it. It is the light flowing from the Sun of Righteousness that alone can make manifest the work of the Holy Spirit in our souls. This is one mode by which the Spirit "bears witness with our spirit that we are the sons of God." He reveals Jesus to the believer. Opening, as it were, the casement, uplifting the window, He admits the light that streams from a Divine Sun, and the soul thus illumined, unveils the wealth, and sparkles with the glories that are garnered there—the restored image of God, and the precious, costly, imperishable graces of the Holy Ghost. Go, then, my reader, and tell Jesus the darkness that broods around you, and that conceals all this glory. Ask Him to arise upon your soul with healing on His wings. One ray darting from that Sun—and how soon will that long, dreary, "night of weeping" be succeeded by the bright "morning of joy." "He that followeth me," says the Saviour, "shall not walk in darkness, but shall have the light of life."

Are You Tempted?

I will suppose you, my reader, to be a *tempted soul*—for *temptation* is an essential element in the spiritual discipline of the child of God. "There hath no temptation taken you but such as is common to man." "Though now for a season, if need be, ye are in heaviness through manifold temptations." Through this furnace, more or less heated, all the followers of Jesus pass—they could not be like Him were it not so. He was tempted like as we are, that He might know how to sympathize with us, and we are tempted that we might fly to the asylum of that sympathy. Perhaps you are tempted to distrust God—to question the Saviour's love to you—to oppose the divine will—to fret, and murmur, and repine at the dealings of your Heavenly Father—to doubt the truth of the Bible, to look upon your professed Christianity as a fiction, and upon all your past experience as a lie.

Poor tempted soul, what are you to do? Whither repair? Already you are prepared to succumb to the foe. You have no heart to resist, no skill to fence, no power to vanquish. Satan is too subtle, experienced, and vigilant in this war to be easily foiled or soon overcome. Already your wounded conscience, confidence, and peace, testify to the perseverance and precision with which his "fiery darts" have been winged. Whither, then, will you look? *Go and tell Jesus.* To whom can you more fitly repair for succor in temptation than to the tempted One? Lay all your case before Him. Tell Him how your faith trembles, how your courage fails, how your heart dies within you, and how ready you are to cast away your confidence, and to part with the anchor of your hope. Oh! methinks, that in a moment—

the scene of His own long, weary temptation in the wilderness still vivid in His remembrance—He will open every recess of His loving, gracious, sympathizing heart, and draw you within the blest pavilion until the storm be past. Tempted ones are peculiarly precious to Jesus. It is His own temptation over again, in the persons of His members. And if there be a niche in His heart deeper, warmer, or more sacred than another, it is where He hides and shelters His Satan and sin-tempted disciples.

Are You Tried?

Go and tell Jesus your trials. To whom, as a *tried* Christian, but to Jesus can you go? Oppressed and sorrowful as our humanity is, there is wanting in each and all the tender, disciplined feeling that exactly harmonizes with our own chastened and pensive spirit. We take our sorrow even to a sorrowing believer, and we find his heart so charged with his own personal trial, his mind so perplexed with his own anxieties, or his spirit so bowed under its own concealed dejection, that we shrink from adding one drop to his brimmed cup by pouring into his sad heart the sadness of our own. He is silent of his own grief, but that silence, oh! how expressive!

But there is One to whom you may go, whose sorrows now are all over, and who is prepared to make yours His own. You are tried in your spirit—tried in your principles—tried in your faith—tried in your worldly calling — tried in your spiritual history—tried in your domestic circumstances—tried in those near and dear to you—whither, son, daughter of trial, can you turn but to Jesus? Have you pondered this sacred and precious privilege? Has it ever bethought you to arise in your grief and go and tell Jesus? He was, as you are, a child of sorrow — a man of grief. Smitten, wounded, traduced, belied, foully accused, bruised, and heart-broken —and is fitted, as no other being in the universe is, to listen to the story of your trial, succor, soothe, and sanctify it.

Are You Bereaved?

These pages will, doubtless, find their way within the home of the —*bereaved.* We refer to this sorrow with the most profound awe— we touch it with a shrinking hand. It seems almost too sacred for human sympathy to approach. But there is One, and only one, who can approach it; One, and only one, who can enter into and understand it; One, and only one, who can soothe it. It is Jesus! Contemplate Him in the bereaved home of of Bethany! Martha and Mary are mourners. Lazarus their brother is dead. Jesus, their brother's Friend and theirs, is come—but He has come too late! "Lord, if thou hadst been here, my brother had not died." No! not too late! It was just the moment that Jesus should come. He timed His visit of sympathy and help with their grief and need. Beloved, Jesus never approaches you a moment sooner, or a moment later than your case demands. He *will come* —but it will be at the *very instant* that you most need Him. There shall be more than an angel's chime of His sympathy with your sorrow —the most perfect and exquisite blending. If He come a moment too soon, your grief would not be matured enough for His sympathy; if a moment too late, that grief might have crushed you. Now, mark the thoughtfulness and skill, the delicacy and sympathy of Jesus. All is inscribed in one brief but expressive sentence: "JESUS WEPT!" To this weeping Jesus go! You return to the house of mourning from the grave where repose the ashes of one once animated and glowing with a spirit that blended with your own—you seem to have entombed a second self—all that gave existence an object, or life its charm. But rise, and go to Jesus. Tell Him what a wreck your heart is, what a blank life seems, and what wintry gloom enshrouds all the landscape of human existence. Tell Him how mysterious to your view seems the event—how heavy falls the blow—what hard, dark, rebellious thoughts of God now haunt your perturbed mind. Lay your grief upon Jesus' breast. Think not that you are alone in your sorrow—that there is not one in this wide, wide world, one who can appreciate your loss, or enter into all the peculiar features of your afflictions, the delicate shadings of your sadness; Jesus can, and Jesus only. The vacancy, too, death has made, in your love and friendship, whatever be the relation, Jesus can fill. Ah! there is not a relation, many and varied though they are, both of domestic and social life, which the Son of God has not assumed, so that when these human ties are sundered by death, Jesus stands prepared to reknit, replace, and restore them, by Himself occupying the vacancy. In the rupture of the parental bond, He is a *Father;* of the filial, He is a *Son ;* of the conjugal, he is a *Husband ;* of the fraternal, He is a *Brother ;* of friendship, He is *Friend.* Thus, in every condition of human life, whatever the peculiarity of its bond, the specialty of its sorrow, or the desolation it produces, Jesus avows His aptitude and readiness to meet and sympathize with it. Go, then, bereaved mourner, and present your claim to a new-born relation, it may be, to the Incarnate Son of God.

Are You in a Strait?

It is possible that you are entangled within the meshes of a present *difficulty*, to the unravelment of which no clue presents itself, and from which there appears no way of escape. Human ingenuity is baffled, creature strength fails, all earthly means are exhausted, and you are at your wits' end. Behold your remedy, how near, how simple—*go and tell Jesus.* Take your difficulty and spread it before the Lord. Your appeal to His compassion, and your believing reliance upon His promise, will secure on your behalf infinite wisdom and omnipotent strength. Listen to the divine declaration, simple faith in which will raise you above your circumstances: "Behold, I am the Lord, the God of all flesh: *is any thing too hard for me?*" Then, what is your present entanglement, great though it be, to Him, "with whom nothing is impossible"? In a moment, and by a way transcending all your thoughts and conceptions, He can "pluck your feet out of the net," and bring you into a "large place where there is no straitness." Pore not despairingly over your obstacles, faint not under your adversity, sit not down, stunned and paralyzed, upon the stone of difficulty, asking, "Who will roll it away?"—here is your effectual remedy, adopt it in faith and you shall be delivered—*go and tell Jesus.* Enlist Him on your side, retain Him as your Counsellor, honor Him by committing your case to His skill, power, and willingness, and He will guide you through all the intricacies of your position, making the rough path smooth, and the crooked path straight. Jesus has power to rescue you from all your entanglements. He can level the mountain, lift up the valley, roll aside the rock, and clear your way to an equitable, honorable, and happy adjustment of all your worldly difficulties. Only make use of Him. Only honor Him. Only confide in Him. Only call upon Him. All hearts are in His hand, all resources are at His command, all agencies are at His disposal; nothing is impossible with Jesus but to *deny Himself* — this He *can not* do. Then, "be careful for nothing, but in every thing by prayer and supplication with thanksgiving, *let your requests be made known unto God.*"

Tell Jesus Every Thing.

What more shall we say? We will sum up all in a few words—Go and tell Jesus *every thing.* You have much to disclose—tell Him all. Tell Him of the world's woundings, of the saints' smitings, of the spirit's tremblings, and of the heart's anguish. Tell Him your low frames, your mental despondencies, your gloomy fears, beclouded evidences and veiled hope. Tell Him your bodily infirmities — your waning health, failing vigor, progressive disease—the pain, the lassitude, the nervousness, the weary couch, the sleepless pillow, which no one knows but Him. Tell Him of your dread of death, how you recoil from dying, and how dark and rayless appears the body's last resting-place. Tell Him how all beyond it looks so dreary, starless, hopeless. Tell Him you fear you do not know Him, love Him, believe in Him. Tell Him that there is not a being in the universe — none in heaven or on earth — whom you desire as Himself. Tell Him all the temptations, the difficulties, the hidden trials and sorrows of your path—tell, oh! tell Him *all!* There is nothing that you may not in the confidence of love, and in the simplicity of faith, tell Jesus — no temporal want—no spiritual sorrow. "Casting *all* your care upon him, for he careth for you." "Ye people, *pour out your heart* before him!" Tell Him your desolateness as a widow—your friendlessness as an orphan—your sadness and solitude as one whose heart is overwhelmed within you. Go, and lose yourself in the love of Jesus—hide you in the wounds of Jesus—wash you in the blood of Jesus—replenish you from the fullness of Jesus, and recline upon the bosom of Jesus. Think not this a weak, sentimental Christianity to which we are urging you. We know no other than this—no other which so appeals to the intellect, as to the most sacred feelings and affections of the heart. This telling Jesus every thing in our individual history—this recognition of His government in all our ways, and this reliance upon His power and love in all our circumstances—is the legitimate employment of a faith at once the sublimest exercise of the mind as it is the loveliest and holiest impulse of the heart. Here is a faith that recedes from the objects of sense, and "beholds Him that is invisible;" that quits the region of illusions and shadows, and entwines itself with infinite realities; that carries all the interests and relations, responsibilities and accountabilities of time into the solemn, awful, and unalterable decision of eternity. In urging you, Christian reader, to the exercise of a privilege of personal contact and close transaction with Jesus, we have but endeavored to simplify a principle, in its application to all the minutiæ of life, the divinest, loftiest, and sublimest that can possibly task the powers of the human soul. All the splendor of human philosophy, science, and prowess, pales before the moral grandeur which gathers, like a halo, around a mortal man reposing at the feet of the Incarnate God—unveiling his whole soul in all the childlike confidence of a faith that grasps Jehovah. At this focal point must meet the profound philosopher and the untutored peasant; the matured man and the little child—all taught, counselled, and supplied at the feet of Jesus.

It only remains that we briefly glance at the *sanctifying influence* this operation of faith must naturally exert.

Intimacy with Christ.

The first result to which we refer is, *the close intimacy with Christ* which the habit cultivates. Human society will illustrate this. It is close intercourse with our fellow-beings that removes ignorance, dissolves prejudice, and unseals in our hearts the hidden springs of confidence, affection, and sympathy. How many of the Lord's people stand aloof from each other's society simply from not knowing one another. Did believers in the Lord Jesus more frequently meet in council, in service, in communion, how soon and entirely would the coldness, the party-spirit, the jealousies, the erroneous impressions vanish which now, alas! divide the body of Christ, all whose members are "members one of another." Knowing each other better, they would love each other more; and loving each other more, there would be more ready concession made to the freedom of judgment and the claims of conscience. The clergy of the various sections of the Christian Church stand too wide apart from each other simply because they do not know each other. And if the shepherds are thus sundered, it is no marvel that the sheep are divided! The Church of Christ is *essentially* one, why should she not be *visibly* one? Inseparable from Christ, why should we be separated from each other? With an essential unity of faith, why should we not all unite in excluding uncharitableness? Oh! if the Lord's people—losing sight of every badge but Christian, and of every name but Christ—were to mingle more frequently, confidingly, and prayerfully together, how much more would they find of assimilation, of sympathy, and affection—how much less to sunder, separate, and censure, and how much more to admire, love, and imitate in each other than they had any conception of. "I believe in the communion of saints" —would then be, not a cold, heartless, unbelieving acknowledgment of a creed, but the sincere, glowing avowal of a fact! Apply this to our intercourse with Jesus. It would be impossible for us to cultivate the habit of telling Him every sin, every sorrow, every temptation, every trial, in a word, every incident of every hour of our daily history, and not increase in a knowledge of Christ. We should then "grow up *into Christ* in all things." The flower absorbs the light, the heat, the air, the dew, and *so* maintains its vitality, unfolds its beauty, and breathes its fragrance. It is by a similar absorption of Christ into our souls that we grow, becoming vigorous, holy, and fruitful. "He that dwelleth in me and I in him the same bringeth forth much fruit; for without me ye can do nothing." Oh! how endeared will Christ become, and God our Father in Him, by this habit of going and telling Jesus every thing. The more frequently we go to Jesus the more intimately we shall know Him; and the more intimately we know Him, the more ardently shall we love, self-denyingly serve, and closely resemble Him. Oh! how close, confiding, and endearing will your intimacy become by this habit of going and telling Him every thing! How will His glory, loveliness, and excellence unfold to your admiring eye. Day by day, and hour by hour, each exigence of its history will reveal stronger reason wherefore you should admire, love, trust, and glorify Christ. Language can not describe how growingly precious He will become to your soul; how more intensely your heart's affections will clasp and firmly entwine around Him, your whole soul striving day by day to please and glorify Him here, longing to be with Him that you might see and enjoy Him hereafter forever.

The Strengthening of Faith.

This habit, too, will greatly tend to *the nourishing and strengthening of faith.* It is faith that takes us to Jesus, and each fresh act of faith invigorates the divine principle. Faith, taking every thing to Christ, and bringing back every thing from Christ, by this process "groweth exceedingly." Would you, my reader, have a faith powerful and stalwart, a faith that can slay the vaunting foe with a pebble and a sling, that demurs not at probabilities or impossibilities, because it leans upon Him with whom all things are possible, then you must have close transactions with Jesus, the "Author and Finisher of your faith." The eaglet's eye acquires strength of vision by gazing upon the sun—thus will your eye of faith be strengthened by "looking unto

Jesus," the "Sun of Righteousness," *in* every thing, and *for* every thing.

This habit of continuous application to the Lord Jesus *will keep your heart as an evergreen planted by the water-courses.* The springs of its devotion will be kept pure and flowing; its affections fresh and ascending. My reader, true godliness has its empire *in the heart.* As a man's heart, so is he. It is the moral mainspring of the soul—it regulates and governs the whole man. Oh! watch with sleepless vigilance, with the most prayerful interest, the power of godliness in your heart. Let other religious professors, if they will, split hairs and solve abstract problems in theology. Let them speculate and refine, spending their energies and time in upraising but the scaffolding of the building—let the religion of others more consist in frivolous conversation, heartless levity, and unholy gossip about preachers and preaching, churches and societies — criticising, fault-finding, condemning— with you, my Christian reader, let the one, grand, momentous, absorbing matter be—the religion of God in your soul—the making sure work for eternity. A religious professor may talk about ministers and churches, and parishes, and societies all his life, and be lost forever! Alas! alas! it is with a mournful and solemn conviction of its truth we pen it — the religion of thousands, and of tens of thousands, has no more spiritual vitality than this! Why is it that in the professing Church of God there is so much vain conversation, idle, worldly gossip—so much evil-speaking and backbiting — so much censoriousness, suspicion, and condemning?

Alas! it is because there exists so little real, Christ-like godliness in those who profess it. Why is it that there is so little of the meekness and gentleness of Christ, of the spirit of charity, kindness, and forbearance—the taking the low place—the refusal to join others in hurling the missile, in uncovering the infirmity, and in inflaming the wound of a Christian brother or sister? alas! it is because multitudes who, though professing His name, have no close, heart-transactions with Jesus. The more closely you deal with Christ, the more faithfully you will deal with *yourself*, and the less inclination and time you will have to deal with others. You will feel that to "save *yourself*," were a matter sufficiently momentous to absorb every feeling, and thought, and moment; and that, having made sure of this, all the time and energy and sympathy you have to spare would find its appropriate work in endeavoring to "save others." How is it, then, with you, my reader? Is that kingdom of Jesus, which "cometh not with observation," which "consisteth not in meats and in drinks, but in righteousness, joy, and peace in the Holy Ghost," dwelling, advancing, ascending in you? Are you a *living* soul—enshrining a *living* Christ—yielding in your life the fruit of a *living* faith, and cherishing a *living* hope of *life eternal?* What present transactions have you with Jesus—in your closet, by the wayside, in your families, and amid the din and conflict of your worldly calling? *This* will be the test and gauge of the reality and depth of your Christianity—*your personal dealings with Christ.*

Honoring Jesus.

The crowning blessing accruing from this sacred privilege is — *the praise, honor, and glory it will bring to Jesus.* To secure this as its end were worth embarking in any labor, with any self-denial, and at any cost. To plant one gem in His crown — to blend one note in the anthem of His praise — to add one beam to the sun of His glory— oh! ten thousand lives spent, ten thousand deaths endured, were as nothing! Conceive, if it be possible, what a continuous revenue of glory is accruing to Jesus from your constant habit of conferring with Him—communing with Him—drawing from Him in all the minute concerns of daily life. Each occasion that you repair to confess at His cross — to draw from His fullness — to lay your grief upon His sympathy—to confide in His counsel—to repose in His love, and to spread around you the adamant shield of His power, you place a fresh diadem upon His head—that head that will ere long appear in the clouds of heaven, wearing and radiant with His "many crowns."

Live in the constant expectation of soon seeing Him face to face—conversing with whom here below, cheered, beguiled, and sweetened many a weary step of your Christian pilgrimage. That moment is speeding on. In a little while and all that now wounds and ruffles, tempts and pollutes, will have disappeared like the foam upon the billow, and you shall eternally repose your weary soul in the bosom of Jesus.

"A little while to wear the robe of sadness,
To walk with weary feet through thorny ways,

Then to pour forth the fragrant oil of
gladness,
And clasp the girdle round the robe of
praise."

Are you, reader, entering upon the New Year still *unconverted?* Oh! we beseech you, begin it with contrition, confession, and prayer at the Cross. Dare not to add another year of impenitence, unbelief, and sin to the many which have gone before to judgment. Seek the "washing of regeneration," which is, "the renewing of the Holy Ghost," without which you can not enter into the kingdom of glory. Seek it with all your heart, and seek it NOW.

Forward, believer in Christ, to the toils, duties, and trials of another stage of life's journey! Christ is enough for them all, and Christ will be with you in them all, and Christ will triumphantly conduct you through them all. Begin your year —telling Jesus; continue it—telling Jesus; close it—telling Jesus. Imitate the early Christians, who, at the termination of their day of labor, "gathered themselves unto Jesus, *and told him* all things, both what they had done, and what they had taught." Tell Jesus you have no grace but what He communicates—no strength but what He gives—no love but what He inspires —no sympathy but what He vouchsafes. Then will come His sweet and instant response: "Dost thou hang upon me, my loved disciple, for all? Then all benediction shall be thine, and thine forever!"

One word ere we close. Do not dishonor the Lord by repairing to human counsel and sympathy first, and failing, then betake yourself to Him. Many Christians are ruled by this principle of making Christ secondary and subordinate to the creature, greatly to their own loss and His discredit. But in all things, in all teaching, in all service, in all obedience, yea, in all your ways, give Jesus the *preëminence.* He asks it — expects it — and is most worthy of it. Go and tell Jesus *first.* Make Him your confident before the creature. The bereaved disciples betook them to no mere human sympathy. They went sad and lonely from the grave of their Master to the bosom of their Lord, and buried their sorrow in His loving, sympathizing heart. Imitate their Christ-honoring example. Ere you take counsel of man, or ask sympathy of friendship — ere you confer and communicate with the dearest and nearest earthly friend— go and tell Jesus. Thus confiding in Him, He will return your confidence a thousandfold. Pleased with your dependence, honored by your trust, and moved by your appeal, He will graciously respond: "Thou art my servant, I have chosen thee, and not cast thee away; fear thou not; for I am with thee: be not dismayed, for I am thy God. I will strengthen thee: yea, I will help thee; yea, I will uphold thee with the right hand of my righteousness." Enough! my gracious Lord! Enough! Arise, my soul!

Go and Tell Jesus!

O Lord! how happy is the time,
When in Thy love I rest;
When from my weariness I climb
E'en to thy tender breast.
The night of sorrow endeth there,
Thy rays outshine the sun;
And in Thy pardon, and Thy care,
The heaven of heavens is won.

"Let the world call itself my foe,
Or let the world allure;
I care not for the world—*I go*
To this tried Friend and sure.
And when life's fiercest storms are sent
Upon life's wildest sea,
My little bark is confident,
Because it holds by Thee.

"When the law threatens endless death,
Upon the dreadful hill,
Straightway from its consuming breath
My soul mounts higher still;

She hastes to Jesus, wounded, slain,
And finds in Him her home,
Whence she shall not go forth again,
And where no death can come.

"I do not fear the wilderness,
Where Thou hast been before:
Nay! rather would I daily press
After Thee! near Thee, more!
Thou art my strength, on Thee I lean,
My heart Thou makest sing;
And to Thy pastures green at length
Thy chosen flock wilt bring.

"And if the gate that opens there
Be closed to other men,
It is not closed to those who share
The heart of Jesus then.
That is not losing much of life,
Which is not losing Thee,
Who art as present in the strife,
As in the victory!

"Therefore, how happy is the time,
When in Thy love I rest,
When from my weariness I climb,
E'en to Thy tender breast.
The night of sorrow endeth there,
Thy rays outshine the sun,
And in Thy pardon and Thy care,
The heaven of heavens is won!"

From the German of Dresler

www.ingramcontent.com/pod-product-compliance
Lightning Source LLC
LaVergne TN
LVHW011121110826
845150LV00008B/2209

* 9 7 8 1 4 2 5 5 0 2 3 5 5 *